Hockey

trailblazers

Nicole Mortillaro

Scholastic Canada Ltd.

Toronto   New York   London   Auckland   Sydney
Mexico City   New Delhi   Hong Kong   Buenos Aires

Scholastic Canada Ltd.
604 King Street West, Toronto, Ontario M5V 1E1, Canada

Scholastic Inc.
557 Broadway, New York, NY 10012, USA

Scholastic Australia Pty Limited
PO Box 579, Gosford, NSW 2250, Australia

Scholastic New Zealand Limited
Private Bag 94407, Botany, Manukau 2163, New Zealand

Scholastic Children's Books
Euston House, 24 Eversholt Street, London NW1 1DB, UK

Library and Archives Canada Cataloguing in Publication
Mortillaro, Nicole, 1972-
Hockey trailblazers / Nicole Mortillaro.
ISBN 978-1-4431-0469-2
1. Hockey players--Biography--Juvenile literature. 2. National Hockey League--
Biography--Juvenile literature. 3. Role models-- Biography--Juvenile literature. I. Title.
GV848.5.A1M67 2011   j796.962092'2   C2010-906020-2

6 5 4 3 2 1   Printed in Singapore 46   11 12 13 14 15

CONTENTS

To my daughter, Sara, and to those who have never let the word "impossible" slow them down.

— N.M.

INTRODUCTION

"Impossible."

That word can mean different things to different people. To some, it means giving up on a dream. To others, it just means trying harder.

Hockey is a Canadian tradition, and playing in the NHL has been the dream of generations of Canadian kids. But for many, playing the sport at the highest levels isn't easy. They have been told that because of what they are, it is impossible.

Here are the stories of five leaders in the sport of hockey — people who didn't believe in the word "impossible"; who overcame challenges to play the game at the highest possible level. These players were truly trailblazers — they created a path so that they, and those who followed, could play the game they loved.

WILLIE O'REE

William Eldon O'Ree was born on October 15, 1935, the youngest of 13 children. Canada was a very different place back then. There wasn't the mix of cultures there is today. In fact, there were only two black families in Fredericton, New Brunswick, when Willie was growing up there. The families even lived on the same street.

Willie loved sports. He played rugby and baseball at school. But it was hockey that grabbed hold of his heart. He started skating at age three and was playing in a league at five. Willie's brother Richard passed on his love of hockey to his younger brother. Richard even tried to teach Willie how to toughen up.

"I remember a couple of times that he would smash me into the boards, a clean check," Willie recalls. "Sometimes the tears would come to my eyes and I would say, 'Brother, why are you hitting me so hard?' and he'd say, 'I just want to let you know, if you plan to play professionally one day . . . you'll be hit a lot harder than this.'"

Willie continued to try to be the best at the sport he loved the most. By the time he was 14, he wondered if he had what it would take to play in the NHL.

Although O'Ree was a talented player, with a burst of speed and good agility, fans weren't used to seeing a black player on the ice. Fans would call him names from the stands. Some even threw things at him. But he never gave up and played as strong as ever.

But in his last year in junior hockey, O'Ree suffered a serious injury. He was positioned in front of the net and was cross-checked from behind. He turned to look at his opponent. As he turned back to see where the puck was going, it hit him right in the face. It broke his nose and part of his jaw.

O'Ree lost almost 95% of the vision in his right eye. The doctor told him that he would never play hockey again. But he got out of the hospital and started skating that same day. He was determined to go on. Nothing was going to stop Willie O'Ree from doing what he loved.

O'Ree played for the Fredericton Junior Capitals in 1951–52 and 1952–53 before joining the Senior Capitals.

"I still had one good eye," he said.

O'Ree returned to playing hockey, and he kept his vision loss to himself. Why fight a battle against racism *and* being partially blind?

And he was good — even with just one working eye. He moved up through the hockey ranks quickly. As a winger for the Fredericton Capitals in the New Brunswick Senior Hockey league, he helped lead his team to the 1954 Allan Cup. He joined the Quebec Frontenacs the next season, and they won the Memorial Cup.

O'Ree joined the Ontario Hockey Association's Junior A Kitchener Canucks the following season. He scored 30 goals. This was his best performance yet.

But despite his hockey success he still loved baseball, too, and he thought about giving that sport a chance. He went to Atlanta, Georgia, in the United States to try out for the Milwaukee Braves. Once there, he experienced racism unlike any that he'd ever faced.

Can you play hockey if you can't hear? Jim Kyte knows you can. Kyte became the first deaf NHL player when he laced up for the Winnipeg Jets in 1982. He was born with a hereditary disease and began losing his hearing when he was just three years old.

"My dad always said, 'It may be a handicap, but it's not a disability,'" he recalls. "You should be able to do anything you want to if you work hard enough at it and have the passion for it." And Kyte did. He went on to become a well-known hockey tough guy. He didn't let his inability to hear slow him down. He wore a special helmet that protected his hearing aids. Because he couldn't hear his teammates call out to him, he would lip-read. And when playing against the boards, he looked at the glass instead of through it to see who was behind him.

Kyte retired from the NHL in 1997, when a

car accident ended his career and left him with permanent post-concussion syndrome. But Kyte overcame this challenge too. He is now a professor of Sport Business Management and a motivational speaker.

"I'd never been in the South before, so I fly into Atlanta and step off the plane and went into the terminal and the first thing I saw was 'White Only' and 'Coloured Only' restrooms," he remembers. When he was made to ride at the back of the bus, he started rethinking his choice to play baseball professionally. He decided to head back home to Canada.

"I sat on the back of the bus, which I was not accustomed to, being from Canada, where I could sit anywhere on the bus. As we're getting farther up north I start moving up on the bus," he recalls. "By the time I got to Bangor, Maine, I was sitting right in front of the bus. When I got back to my hometown I said, 'Willie, forget about baseball, concentrate on playing hockey.'"

Upon his return, O'Ree almost turned down the opportunity to join a professional league. But the coach of the Quebec Aces, Punch Imlach — who would one day coach the Toronto Maple Leafs to several Stanley Cups — persuaded him to sign with his team. The

O'Ree went pro with the Quebec Aces in 1956.

Aces won the league title. Later, O'Ree played for the
Springfield Indians. While there, his shining moment
came. The Boston Bruins noticed his performance and
called him up to play an NHL game.

On January 18, 1958, Willie O'Ree stepped on to the ice at the Montreal Forum in his Boston Bruins uniform. The moment wasn't marked by any special applause or ceremony. O'Ree took his place like every other player. Yet that moment would go down in hockey history. Willie O'Ree had become the first black player to take part in an NHL game.

"It was the greatest thrill of my life," he said at the time. "I'll always remember this day."

O'Ree (far left) plays in his second NHL game, against the Toronto Maple Leafs, on January 7, 1961.

Looking back, O'Ree said, "It was just a great feeling. I didn't get any goals, no assists, didn't get into any fights, nothing. But we beat the Canadiens 3–0. Shut them out, right in Montreal."

O'Ree only ended up playing in two games for the Bruins that season. He returned to the minors. In 1961, he was called back up and played in another 43 games for the Bruins, scoring 4 goals and 10 assists.

But it didn't matter how good a player he was — racism was still a problem for O'Ree.

"In the penalty box, stuff would be thrown at you . . . they'd spit at me," he said.

But O'Ree didn't let it get to him.

"I never fought one time because of racial remarks. I fought because guys butt-ended me and speared me and cross-checked me and things of this nature. I fought because I had to, not because I wanted to."

The media started calling him "the Jackie Robinson of hockey."

Willie O'Ree and Jackie Robinson

When Willie O'Ree was 14, he played in a baseball tournament. The winning team was taken to New York. One of the things they did was to go to a Brooklyn Dodgers game, where O'Ree got the chance to meet Jackie Robinson.

Just a year earlier, Robinson had become the first black man in Major League Baseball. Before then only white players were allowed in the league, and many people did not want to allow black players. Robinson "broke the colour barrier" and went on to become a superstar.

"I told him, 'Mr. Robinson, I play hockey, too,'" O'Ree recalled. "He asked me, 'Black kids play hockey?'" When O'Ree met Jackie Robinson again in 1962, he was happily surprised to find that the baseball star remembered him.

"When I played, I knew I was a black man. Nobody had to tell me that. So when I went out and played, I just wanted to be accepted as just another player."

Although O'Ree still faced some taunts from fans and even opposing players, he remained in hockey and had a very successful career in the minors. He may not have played long in the NHL, but it didn't matter: he had paved the way for black players in hockey.

It wasn't until 13 years later that Mike Marson became the second black player in the NHL. But he was followed by many more, including such superstars as Grant Fuhr and Jarome Iginla. In the past 50 years, more than 40 black players have played in the NHL.

Willie O'Ree has since gone on to work for the NHL's diversity program, called "Hockey Is for Everyone," as its Director of Youth Development. This program encourages children to take part in hockey no matter what their background or abilities.

Speaking about the NHL's diversity program, O'Ree says, "We're trying to reach out and touch as

O'Ree addresses the media at the 1998 NHL All-Star Game in Vancouver.

many boys and girls as possible and let them know that there's another sport that they can play."

In 2010 O'Ree received the Order of Canada, joining the ranks of such NHL greats as Gordie Howe, Wayne Gretzky and Jean Béliveau in receiving the honour.

O'Ree once said, "You can do anything you set your mind to do; if you feel strongly within your heart, within your mind, you can do it."

Jarome Iginla

Jarome Iginla, captain of the Calgary Flames, was the first black player to win the Maurice Richard Trophy for having the most regular-season goals in the NHL. Although he grew up hearing that there weren't many black players in the NHL, he never gave up. He looked to pioneers like Willie O'Ree and to his favourite player, Grant Fuhr, for inspiration.

"To see the first black player to ever play the game is pretty inspiring," Iginla said about O'Ree.

Iginla (right) with Simon Gagné (left) and Joe Sakic (centre) with their gold medals at the 2002 Winter Olympics

GEORGE ARMSTRONG
Centre
TORONTO MAPLE LEAFS

George Armstrong

Hockey has been popular in Canada for well over a hundred years, not only with the English and French Canadians who had settled here, but with Native people. In fact, there are many similarities between hockey and lacrosse, the popular Aboriginal summer game that is Canada's other national sport.

Many First Nations communities have their own teams and tournaments, but, perhaps surprisingly, there haven't been a lot of Native players in the NHL. One player who led the way for people of Aboriginal descent was George Armstrong.

George Edward Armstrong was born on July 6, 1930 in Skead, Ontario. He was of Irish and Algonquin heritage. As with many boys his age in Northern Ontario, he had a keen love of hockey. He would often play on the local rinks, trying to improve his skills.

George was a big boy, and solid. By the time he was 16 years old he was playing for the Copper Cliff Redmen, along with future Toronto Maple Leaf great Tim Horton. In the 1946–47 season with the Redmen, he scored 6 goals and 5 assists in just 9 games. NHL scouts started to take notice of the young man. The Toronto Maple Leafs put him on their protected list, which meant that they wanted to draft him.

The next season the Leafs' Junior A team in Stratford, Ontario, needed a player. The Leafs sent

Armstrong. There he led the league in scoring with 73 points in just 36 games, and won the league's most valuable player award. Once the Leafs signed him the following season, Armstrong played on their junior affiliate team, the Toronto Marlboros of the Ontario Hockey Association, where he could hone his skills. He was soon moved up to play with the senior Toronto Marlboros of the American Hockey League.

While he was with the senior Marlboros the

Armstrong played for both the junior Marlies, where he was captain, and the senior team. Many years later he coached the senior Marlies to the Memorial Cup.

team played in a tournament at the Stoney Indian Reserve in Alberta. When the people there heard about Armstrong's Native heritage, they called him "Chief Shoots-the-Puck" and gave him a ceremonial headdress. The name stuck, and Armstrong was dubbed "Chief" by his teammates — not only for his heritage, but for his leadership qualities.

Armstrong played most of the next few seasons for the Pittsburgh Hornets, the Leafs' American Hockey League farm team.

On December 3, 1949, Armstrong stepped onto the ice at Maple Leaf Gardens to play in an NHL game for the first time. He played his second game on December 24, and although he didn't get any points, his presence on the ice was felt.

The rest of that season and the following one, he mainly played for the Hornets. In 1951–52 he was called back up to play for the Leafs again. He played in 20 games and managed to get his first goal. The *Toronto Daily Star* recorded the historic occasion: "His goal was a lulu. He took Bentley's pass in full flight, brushing big Butch Bouchard aside as he stormed around him, then fired a low one that McNeil got his skate on but couldn't handle. Big George jumped two feet in the air, let go a war-whoop that was drowned in the tremendous cheer that greeted the rookie's goal." That would go down not only as the winning goal, but also as the first goal ever scored by a Native player in the NHL.

The following season, Armstrong joined the Leafs

Armstrong signs a contract as his mother and Conn Smythe look on.

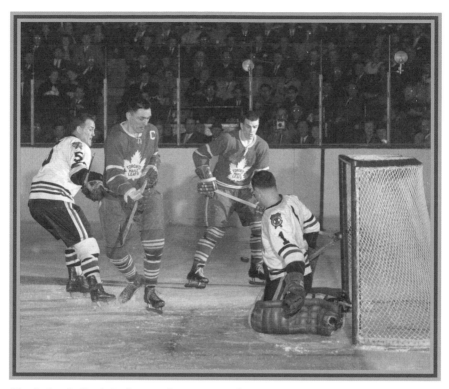

Maple Leafs Captain George Armstrong tries to score against Glenn Hall of the Chicago Black Hawks.

full-time. He was never a fast skater or a big goal-scorer but Armstrong was good, and he was an excellent leader. In 1957–58 he was named team captain.

"The Chief" went on to lead the Maple Leafs to four Stanley Cups in five years. He became longest-serving captain in Leafs history, and was inducted into the Hockey Hall of Fame in 1975.

Fred Sasakamoose

At the same time as George Armstrong was making his way through the NHL, another Aboriginal player was making his mark on the sport. Frederick Sasakamoose was born on December 24, 1934, in Sandy Lake Reserve, Saskatchewan. He first began playing hockey at residential school. His love of hockey and his skill took him to the Moose Jaw Canucks of the Western Canada Junior Hockey League in 1950. In his final season with the Canucks, he scored 31 goals in just 34 games. He went on to be named the Most Valuable Player in the league that year.

In 1954, Fred Sasakamoose achieved a dream: he was drafted by the Chicago Black Hawks, and on February 27 he took to the ice at Maple Leaf Gardens for his first game.

"The greatest moment of my life, when I stepped [out] at Toronto Maple Leaf Gardens," he said. *That night legendary sportscaster Foster Hewitt met with Sasakamoose to ask him how to pronounce his name. He also asked Sasakamoose if he minded being called Indian. "No, I'm proud to be an Indian. I'm proud of who I am," he said.*

Sasakamoose played in 11 NHL games that season. He returned to the minors, where he played for six more seasons. After he retired from hockey, Sasakamoose created hockey schools for aboriginal youth and worked for the NHL's diversity program, to continue inspiring aboriginal players.

Armstrong signing autographs for two young fans

Since aboriginal players like George Armstrong and Fred Sasakamoose led the way with their determination and skill, many others have pursued careers in hockey, including recent NHL players like René Bourque, Jonathan Cheechoo and Sheldon Souray.

Hoisting the Stanley cup in 1963

Jordin Tootoo became the first NHL player of Inuit descent when he played his first game for the Nashville Predators on October 9, 2003. Tootoo's mother is of Irish descent and his father is Inuk, from Nunavut. Although he was born in Churchill, Manitoba, he grew up in Rankin Inlet, Nunavut. Tootoo has gone on to inspire other Inuit children to pursue their dreams. He was presented with a National Aboriginal Achievement Award in 2002 and is featured on posters encouraging kids to stay in school and set goals.

MANON RHÉAUME

On September 23, 1992, the Tampa Bay Lightning goalie skated out from behind the net for the warm-up at the Florida State Fairgrounds Expo Hall. A little smaller than most, the goalie was greeted with whistles and cheers from the stands. This was an historic event. It was, after all, the first time a woman was playing in an NHL uniform.

Manon Rhéaume was born on February 24, 1972, in Lac Beauport, Quebec. She learned to skate when she was three years old. But the town didn't have a league of its own, so Manon's father decided to make an outdoor rink and create one.

Manon saw the other kids playing. Her father played hockey and her brothers played hockey. At age five she decided that she, too, wanted to play. Since nobody wanted to play in goal, she gladly donned the pads.

As she grew up, Manon's interest in hockey didn't waver. She continued to play, always with boys, as she rose up through the different levels of hockey. There simply weren't any girls' leagues for her to play in.

When she was 11, she played in the International Pee Wee Hockey Tournament in Quebec. This was the same tournament that had featured such future NHL greats as Wayne Gretzky, Mario Lemieux and Guy Lafleur. She was the first girl ever to appear in the tournament.

Women in Hockey

Although hockey is popular today with both boys and girls, historically it was thought of as a man's sport. But women were playing the game very early on as well. The Stanley Cup is named after Lord Stanley, but not many people know that his daughter Isobel loved to play hockey. There was a rink on the lawn at Rideau Hall where she regularly played shinny — in a long skirt! The first organized women's hockey game was held at Rideau Hall in 1891.

At 19 years old, Rhéaume played for the Trois-Rivières Draveurs of the Quebec Major Junior Hockey League, against men. Rhéaume was once again knocking down barriers in a male-dominated sport.

Shortly after that, the Tampa Bay Lightning showed interest in the young hockey star. They asked her to play in that historic pre-season game against the St. Louis Blues. She faced 9 shots and made 7 saves. Unfortunately, the team didn't win the game.

Rhéaume practises for her NHL pre-season game against the St. Louis Blues.

In 1955, Abigail Hoffman made a very important move. She loved hockey. But there was nowhere for a girl to play competitively in Toronto. So nine-year-old "Ab" cut her hair and registered in a boys' league. She was a great player. But when she was chosen for an all-star team, she had to show her birth certificate, and her secret was out.

When people discovered that Abby was a girl, she became an instant star. People lined up to interview her and her family, and she was invited by the Montreal Canadiens and Toronto Maple Leafs to meet their teams.

"I defy anyone to pick her out as a girl when the team is on the ice," her coach told the Toronto Star. "She skates like a boy, plays aggressively, meets the players when they come in on defence."

Abby was allowed to finish the season, but then she had to hang up her skates, since there wasn't a

"Ab" played for the St. Catharines Tee Pees of the Little Toronto Hockey League.

girls' league for her to play in. She sued for the right to play and lost.

But Abby didn't give up on sports. She was a swimmer in high school and went on to became a four-time Olympian in track and field. She later become Director of Sport Canada and continued to fight for athletes' rights.

Some thought Rhéaume was just a way for the team to get more publicity. Still, people at the game realized the significance of what they had just watched. As the teams skated off the ice, the spectators rose to their feet for a standing ovation. They knew that Rhéaume's performance on the ice that night would go down in the hockey history books. Later she was offered a contract with the Atlanta Knights, the Lightning's minor

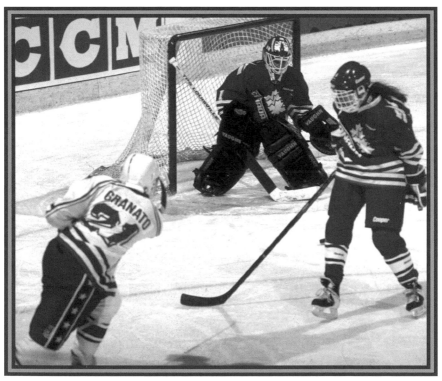

Rhéaume makes a save against Cammie Granato of the USA in the final of the 1994 IIHF World Women's Championship.

league team — another first for a woman.

"I was very nervous," Rhéaume said about the game. "I didn't think about being the first woman. I thought about doing my best and concentrating on the puck."

Rhéaume played for the Atlanta Knights of the International Hockey League in 1992–93.

Rhéaume's hero was NHL great Patrick Roy. She wore number 33 in his honour. And Roy had something to say about her, too: "If Manon becomes an NHL [goalie], I don't think it's going to be because she's a woman; it's because she's got the talent to play there."

Rhéaume went on to play for Canada's National Team. At the 1998 Winter Olympics, when women's hockey first became an Olympic sport, her fantastic play in goal helped the team to win a silver medal.

Rhéaume didn't make it in the NHL. In that, she is no different from many young men. But Rhéaume did

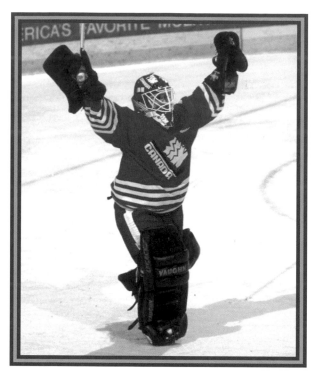

Rhéaume celebrates Canada's win at the 1994 IIHF World Women's Championship.

get to realize a dream by playing in the biggest hockey league in the world, and she made history. In doing so, she paved the way for other girls and young women who might dream of one day playing in the NHL.

"I never thought I could make a trail in the NHL," Rhéaume once said. "I always played because I loved hockey. Hockey for me is a passion. And every time I have a chance to go higher I take the chance."

Hayley Wickenheiser

Hayley Wickenheiser is one of the most talented women in hockey. Some have even referred to her as the female Wayne Gretzky. She became the first woman to score a goal in a men's professional hockey league when she played with the Kirkkonummen Salamat of the Finnish second division league. She also played for a Swedish Division One team. She won an Olympic silver medal in 1998 and went on to win three Olympic golds, in 2002, 2006 and 2010. Hayley has played with such great players as Gillian Apps, Kim St. Pierre and Cassie Campbell, who later became the first woman on the Hockey Night in Canada broadcast.

BOBBY CLARKE

Robert Earle Clarke was like many other boys in Flin Flon, Manitoba: he loved to play hockey. In winter, it was a pretty sure bet that he could be found on the outdoor ice rink at the end of his street.

Bobby also loved watching hockey. He loved to watch his favourite player, Gordie

Howe, as he whipped down the ice. Then, one day, he had a dream come true: Howe played an exhibition game in Flin Flon. As Bobby and his friends stood by the side of the ice, Howe walked by and ruffled his hair.

"It was pretty special," Bobby recalls.

As much as Bobby loved hockey, he hadn't really thought about playing in the NHL. He just wanted to play the game as much as he could.

As he got older, he held on to his love for hockey. He no longer played on an outdoor rink. Instead, he

Bobby Clarke at age 4, in Flin Flon, Manitoba

played for the local team, the Flin Flon Bombers, and he was good.

But when Bobby was 14, he started to notice that he wasn't feeling so well. He was often tired. He was thirsty. And he started to go to the bathroom a lot more often. His mother became worried, so she took him to a doctor.

Bobby didn't really think much of the doctor's tests. They seemed like nothing out of the ordinary. He went home and didn't think about it again. But when the doctor called his mother back to the office later that day, he knew that something had to be wrong.

When they arrived, the doctor broke the news: Bobby had Type 1 diabetes. This was what was making him so tired and thirsty.

Hearing the news didn't change Bobby very much. He didn't tell people about it. To him, it didn't matter. All he cared about was that it didn't stop him from playing hockey.

There are two types of diabetes: Type 1 and Type 2. Type 1 is often called "juvenile diabetes." This is because most people who get it are children.

In Type 1 diabetes, the pancreas no longer makes insulin, which helps our bodies absorb the sugar we have eaten. That means that people with the disease need to inject themselves with insulin every day. Before this treatment was developed, in the 1920s, Type 1 diabetes was a fatal disease. Now, if they are careful, diabetics can live normal lives.

Dr. Charles Best (left) and Dr. Frederick Banting, discoverers of insulin, with a diabetic dog

"I just continued to do the things I'd always done," he said. "It was harder on my mom than it was on me, really."

Clarke had to make sure that the level of sugar in his blood didn't get too low or too high. If it went too low, he could get dizzy and disoriented. If it went too high, he could become disoriented as well, or thirsty and unable to concentrate. At the time, it was not

Clarke played for the Flin Flon Bombers of the Western Canada Junior Hockey League.

as easy for a diabetic to test his blood as it is today. So Clarke had to watch the food he ate. He weighed it and measured it. He needed to keep track of how many grams of carbohydrate (sugars and starches) were in the food. If he knew that, he could give himself the proper amount of insulin. He also had to be very aware of his symptoms.

Clarke continued to play for the Flin Flon Bombers. He loved the action of the game and wasn't afraid to get into the middle of things. His coach, Pat Ginnell, knew he had diabetes, but he didn't treat him any differently. He just made sure that there was cola on the bench in case Clarke's sugar got low.

Clarke's teammates knew that something was going on because of the cola the coach kept around. But, Clarke said, "I didn't look any different, I didn't act any different, so I wasn't treated as different."

Ginnell knew that Clarke was an excellent player and that he had a very good chance of making it in the NHL. But not everyone agreed that

Clarke could make it in the tough league. The NHL scouts who were looking for good players for their teams had heard that Clarke had diabetes. They worried that the tough play in the NHL would be too much for him. They were worried that Clarke could get hurt more easily. They also thought that maybe he just couldn't take the high level of play and might get too tired. The question was, could a player with such a disease make it in the gruelling sport of professional hockey?

Ginnell knew that he had a talented and tough player who could succeed. He took Clarke to the Mayo Clinic, a top hospital in the United States. He had the doctors there examine Clarke. They said that as long as Clarke monitored his blood sugar, there was no reason he couldn't play. Ginnell had them write a letter saying that. When the scouts came around, he showed it to them.

In 1969 Clarke was chosen by the Philadelphia Flyers in the second round of the NHL Draft. This

Clarke's tough style of play on the ice became well known.

was the first time that a player with diabetes had ever been drafted. As if other teams were waiting for someone to show faith in Clarke, the Flyers started to get offers for him right away. Both the Montreal

Chatting with Maurice Richard (right) and Brian McFarlane (left) on **Hockey Night in Canada**

Canadiens and the Detroit Red Wings approached the Flyers. But the Flyers knew they had a good player on their hands. They rejected the offers.

As time went on, it was obvious that the club had made a good choice. Clarke was a great leader on and off the ice. He played for a team that became known for its toughness. In fact, the team was called the "Broad Street Bullies" for their style of play. Diabetes didn't stop Bobby Clarke from fighting hard for the puck or fighting off other players.

Mario Lemieux was an outstanding player for the Pittsburgh Penguins from 1984 to 2006. He was big and strong, and an amazing scorer. But in January 1993, he announced that he had Hodgkin's lymphoma, a type of cancer. Although he was on pace to set Wayne Gretzky's record of 92 goals in a season, he had to step away from the game. But he never once gave up. On the day of his final radiation treatment, he played in a game against the Flyers. He scored a goal and an assist. After the game, the Philadelphia fans gave him a standing ovation. After missing two months of play, he finished second to Gretzky in the scoring race. Lemieux never let his cancer take him away from hockey long.

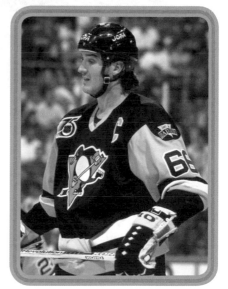

Clarke was made captain of the Flyers in 1973, at just 23 years old. That made him the youngest captain in Flyers history. Clarke also became the first Flyer to win the Bill Masterton Trophy. This trophy goes to the NHL player who "best exemplifies the qualities of perseverance, sportsmanship, and dedication" to hockey.

Clarke played in the Summit Series of 1972, one of the most memorable series in Canadian hockey history. He was the only player to play in all 8 games. It was a hard-fought series, but eventually the Canadians won over the Soviet Union. Clarke faced some heavy criticism for his rough play during that series. Some people thought that he had played unfairly against the Soviets, especially when he slashed their star player.

But after he returned home, Clarke played even better. He had a spectacular NHL career: he won the Hart Memorial Trophy three times (1972, 1975 and 1976). He also won the Lester Patrick Trophy for out-

Clarke battles Alexander Ragulin of the Soviet Union for the puck in Game 2 of the Summit Series.

standing service to hockey in 1976 and the Frank J. Selke Award, which goes to a forward who excels in the defensive aspects of hockey, in 1980. He was named to the First All-Star Team twice (1975 and 1976) and to the Second All-Star Team twice (in 1973 and 1974).

Clarke retired from hockey in 1976 and joined the

As captain of the flyers, Clarke led his team to two Stanley Cup Championships.

front office of the Flyers organization. Today he serves as Senior Vice President of the Flyers.

Bobby Clarke never thought of himself as a

"diabetic player." He thought of himself as a hockey player who happened to have diabetes. He had become the first player in NHL history to play with such a disease. And he proved that it didn't matter — with grit and determination, he faced his challenges and succeeded.

New York Rangers
Rangers de New York

Larry Kwong
Center
Centre

LARRY KWONG

Being called up to play in the NHL is a momen-
tous event. It is the dream of so many young
Canadians — the dream of skating down the
ice with thousands of fans cheering you on.

But what are a player's chances of lasting
in the NHL? Throughout the history of the
league, many men have played just one game,

only to return to the minors. That's exactly what happened to Larry Kwong. So why is he so special?

In 1948, before Willie O'Ree ever thought of playing in the NHL, Larry Kwong helped break a barrier that had existed in hockey since the league's start in 1917. In that time, no Asian player had ever taken to the ice.

Larry was born Eng Kai Geong on June 17, 1923, in British Columbia. His family had immigrated to Canada from China. They owned a store called Kwong Hing Lung and Co. in the small town of Vernon.

Growing up in Canada in the 1920s wasn't easy for a Chinese boy. Chinese-Canadians weren't allowed to vote, and many people wouldn't hire them. It could be hard to do something as simple as find a barber willing to cut your hair.

Larry learned to skate on Vernon's frozen ponds. He started playing hockey when he was seven. His team, the Hydrophones of Vernon, won the BC Midget and Juvenile Championships.

On the 1938–39 Vernon Hydrophones, Kwong was nicknamed "The China Clipper." He powered his team to the BC Provincial Midget Championship.

But playing for the team presented challenges. When they had to travel by car to get to Nelson one winter, their route took them south into the United States. Even though he had his birth certificate with him that showed that he was born in Canada, the American authorities refused to let nine-year-old Larry into the country.

"So, I had to get out of the car, take a train — by myself — and stayed on the Canadian side of the border . . . I did that two times when I was playing juvenile hockey," he says.

"My mother wasn't too much in favour of me playing hockey . . . Chinese people just thought about work. But, I convinced her one day I would make enough money playing hockey to buy her a home."

Even though she wasn't fond of him playing hockey, Larry's mother bought him skates — a few sizes too big. The Kwongs were poor. Larry's father had died when he was just five years old, leaving his mother with 15 children. But every time he'd outgrow a pair of skates, he would cry to his mother for a new pair. Eventually, she would find the money.

Larry's two older brothers encouraged him to play hockey. They told him not to let people's comments discourage him. If he liked hockey, it shouldn't matter if there were other Chinese players or not.

Paul Kariya

Born and raised in North Vancouver, British Columbia, Paul Kariya was the first player of Japanese descent to play in the NHL. He started skating at an early age — but as a figure skater! He started playing hockey a year later. His skating skills were so strong that he quickly moved up and even started playing with older boys. He was drafted, fourth overall, by the Mighty Ducks of Anaheim in 1993 and played on three Canadian Olympic teams, winning gold in 2002.

After high school, Kwong made the legendary Trail Smoke Eaters team. Players were not paid, but the smelting company that owned the team gave the players good jobs. The company refused to hire Kwong at the smelter, though. Instead, the team provided him with a job as a bellhop in a local hotel.

"I would say that hurt. You always remember that," Kwong said.

In 1946 the scout for the New York Rangers saw Kwong play and was impressed. He was invited to the Rangers training camp in Winnipeg and was signed by the team. He played for their farm team, the New York Rovers of the Eastern Hockey League.

Kwong negotiated his own contract. Surprisingly, he believes that he was actually paid more than the average player.

"I was getting six thousand dollars, which was good money for senior hockey in those days," he said. "I got a little bit more — at least, I think I got a little bit more — because I was Chinese, and they thought

Kwong played only one game for the New York Rangers.

that I was more of a drawing [card]."

Kwong said that his teammates were never disrespectful to him.

"The sports people treated me pretty good, actually. The hockey players were very good."

When Kwong appeared in his one and only NHL game at Madison Square Garden on March 13, 1948,

After his stint with the Rangers, Kwong played for the Valleyfield Braves of the Quebec Senior Hockey League for seven seasons.

he was given the key to New York City's Chinatown. In that historic game, Kwong faced the Montreal Canadiens and such superstars as Maurice "Rocket" Richard and Bernie "Boom Boom" Geoffrion.

Larry Kwong played in just one NHL game, although he continued to play hockey until 1957. Still, he took the first step on a path that many other Asian players have followed, including NHL superstar Paul Kariya, David Tanabe, Devin Setaguchi and Richard Park.

Larry Kwong and Trevor Linden at the BC Hockey Hall of Fame Induction Celebration in Penticton, BC, in 2010

These five players did not let anything stand in their way. Not only did they achieve their own dreams of playing in the NHL and internationally, they helped pave the way for others to follow. They faced their obstacles and overcame them.

They never believed in the word "impossible."

INDEX